Emperor Hirohito: The Life and Legacy of Japan's II

By Charles River Editors

A Japanese depiction of the battle

About Charles River Editors

Charles River Editors is a boutique digital publishing company, specializing in bringing history back to life with educational and engaging books on a wide range of topics. Keep up to date with our new and free offerings with this 5 second sign up on our weekly mailing list, and visit Our Kindle Author Page to see other recently published Kindle titles.

We make these books for you and always want to know our readers' opinions, so we encourage you to leave reviews and look forward to publishing new and exciting titles each week.

Introduction

A Japanese depiction of the Samurai's final charge

"It was not clear to me that our course was unjustified. Even now I am not sure how historians will allocate the responsibility for the war." – Emperor Hirohito

The man known to most of the world as Emperor Hirohito ruled during some of the most tumultuous years in Japanese history. When he came to the throne in 1926, he inherited control of a country which had only recently emerged as a major industrial and world power, and through the aggressive expansion and wars of the 1930s, Hirohito was at the head of one of the world's foremost powers. Throughout the maelstrom of World War II, he remained in power, a distant and, to most outsiders, inscrutable factor in the rise of the Japanese Empire.

Before and during the war, many people in America and elsewhere believed that Emperor Hirohito was at least partly responsible for both the confrontational Japanese approach to foreign affairs, and for the often brutal conduct of the Japanese armed forces during the wars which followed. As such, when the war ended, there were plenty of calls for the emperor to be indicted for war crimes along with other senior figures in Japan. However, a new feeling emerged at that time, suggesting that in reality Hirohito had been little more than a figurehead taken along by a tide of militarism, helpless to intervene or influence the course of events.

Modern scholarship suggests that neither of these views of Hirohito is entirely true. At the time he came to the throne, the emperor was revered as a semi-divine figure, and his influence on every level of Japanese political and military life was undeniable and considerable. Although the emperor generally did not express his will through the issuance of direct orders, the displeasure of the emperor was something which every senior member of the military and political sphere sought strenuously to avoid. In this context, to imagine Hirohito as a helpless puppet, a purely constitutional monarch manipulated by ruthless politicians and generals, is an error. Indeed, he was always an active participant in the most important events before and during Japan's war against the Allies. In hindsight, it's clear that the image of Hirohito as a powerless figurehead emerged as part of a legend deliberately created by America and its allies following the war to help maintain a peaceful occupation of Japan. With the dawn of the Cold War, Japan was needed as an ally, allowing it to serve as a potential bulwark against Soviet expansion in Southeast Asia. Rebuilding Japan into a strong and stable power became a priority, and for this, Hirohito was needed to provide continuity and a form of rule to which the Japanese people were accustomed. Thus, Hirohito went on to rule throughout the astonishing Japanese economic recovery in the 1950s and 1960s, all the way until his death in 1989.

The new constitution imposed by America after the war was framed around the monarchy, and to justify keeping Hirohito in power, it was necessary to demonstrate that he had not been personally culpable for Japanese aggression or military brutality. This was so successful that for many years few historians disputed this version of history. It was only relatively recently that new works have concluded that the personality and influence of the Japanese emperor were far greater than this post-war invention suggested. Today, most modern historians agree that Hirohito was neither a helpless dupe nor an aggressive hawk who drove Japan into war - his role was more complex, and his personality played a far more significant role than either of these simplified views would suggest.

Emperor Hirohito: The Life and Legacy of Japan's Ruler during World War II looks at the role of the enigmatic leader in the rise, fall and rebirth of modern Japan. Along with pictures depicting important people, places, and events, you will learn about Emperor Hirohito like never before.

Emperor Hirohito: The Life and Legacy of Japan's Ruler during World War II

About Charles River Editors

Introduction

Free Books by Charles River Editors

Discounted Books by Charles River Editors

The Meiji Restoration and Hirohito's Early Years

The Tokugawa shogunate, a military government under control of a shogun (military dictator) and the last feudal government in Japan, brought an end to the constant civil wars and open warfare of the previous two centuries and ruled for nearly 300 years. Given that it was a military government, military service was critically important to one's social status and essential to occupational classification in the Edo period, making it the perfect age for the samurai.

As a feudal government, the Tokugawa shogunate split control of state domains under feudal lords known as *daimyō*. Although given a high degree of autonomy, the daimyō were responsible to the shogun to provide "maintenance of armed forces, the protection of the coastline, and attendance on the shogun at appointed times."[1] The maintenance of these functions required a large amount of support from society in general, including merchants, peasants, and artisans, but this system of military governance ensured that the warriors' social status was elevated to a position of high prestige. Thus, samurai held a virtual monopoly not only on military positions, but also administrative positions at both the central and regional levels, and as a symbol of their status, samurais were the only class allowed to carry weapons - a longsword and shortsword - in public.

The Tokugawa bureaucracy established a rigid and hierarchical social structure, and Japan severely limited contact with the rest of the world, although it was not the total isolation sometimes presumed. The government was quite aware of what was happening in the rest of the world, and the Japanese left a window open to Europe, in the form of a small and highly restricted Dutch presence on an artificial island in Nagasaki harbor, a presence that lasted more than 200 years. Courtesy of the Dutch, the Japanese were aware of contemporary events in Europe, along with the rest of the world, and they were also aware of scientific and technological progress, although whether this resulted in any practical applications is hard to establish.

There had been a European presence in Japan well before the establishment of the shogun system, resulting in a sizable number of Japanese becoming Catholic Christians, largely through the efforts of Portuguese missionaries. Portuguese and Spanish missionaries had been very active throughout Asia from the early 1500s, so the Japanese were quite aware of the animosity between Dutch Protestants and Iberian Catholics. Under the early shoguns, Christianity was repressed, mostly because the government feared that Christians might aid the Europeans to Japan's detriment. Jesuits, for example, had considerable influence at the Ming Chinese Emperor's court, and eventually, the repression resulted in a Christian rebellion called the Shimabara Rebellion (1637-1638), which was savagely put down. Large numbers of Christians were killed, and while a small Christian presence remained, it only survived underground.

The merits of the Tokugawa period are still debated by historians, but it kept the peace in Japan

---

[1]Jaundrill 2016a:4

for 250 years and prevented the kind of European colonial adventures that bedeviled much of the rest of Asia. Japan famously abandoned guns as weapons, despite arguably having the world's largest number of gunners in the 1590s when it invaded Korea. Japan's central government remained formidable enough to deter European meddling, and European ships attempting to visit Japan were treated harshly.

The Japanese stayed out of the chaos in China as the Ming dynasty collapsed and the Manchu conquerors replaced the Ming dynasty with their own, the Qing, but on July 8, 1853, U.S. Navy Commodore Matthew Perry led four American warships into Uraga Harbor near Edo (later renamed Tokyo), presenting the Japanese with a letter from President Millard Fillmore. The Japanese couldn't know they were at the end of their long withdrawal from the rest of the world, but they were quite aware that the conditions in China and in Asia generally werc being forced to change. They were also certainly aware that the Americans, as a result of the Gold Rush, had made California a state (in 1852) and extended the United States to the Pacific Ocean. They were also aware that American ships dominated the Pacific whaling industry, and that they commonly sailed to China. Japan was further aware of the British and French colonial incursions into China, and they were looking across the Sea of Japan where the Russians were actively occupying territory that was uncomfortably close to Japan. Thus, the appearance of an American naval force was obviously ominous.

Perry

Perry's 1853 flotilla included two sailing ships and two steamships, and Perry returned in February of 1854. The Japanese may not have been very impressed with the gifts from America that Perry presented, but they clearly were impressed by the steamships. Perry's cruises and other threatening events resulted in a fundamental change in Japan, so much so that after having given up guns in the 1600s, the Japanese quickly moved to reintroduce them in the wake of the Americans' arrival.

While there was a debate over how to respond to the Americans, British, French, and Russians, it was obvious to the Japanese that they faced extremely serious threats. As the 19th century wore on, the French empire expanded into what was then called Indochina, taking control of territories that are now Vietnam, Laos and Cambodia, and the British expanded from India into Burma and what is now Malaysia, including areas in Borneo. The Dutch were consolidating their hold on Indonesia, and the Spanish retained their grip on the Philippines. The Russians were flooding into Manchuria and into the Amur region (the Amur River basin, a vast area north of Korea). On top of it all, following the disastrous defeat of the Chinese Qing dynasty during the First Opium War and the weakening of the once formidable dynasty regime by huge rebellions, a number of nations were acquiring concessions in China. The foremost concession went to the British in Hong Kong, but even the Belgians, Austrians, and Italians eventually acquired concessions in China. The Japanese naturally took note.

It became painfully evident that if Japan was to avoid becoming another victim of European colonial expansion, the country would have to become powerful itself. During the 1860s, various conservative daimyō and samurai attacked both the Japanese government and foreigners in a desperate attempt to stop the rolling tide of history and send Japan back into a state of isolation, but in 1868, Japan fully entered the modern age when Emperor Mutsuhito ascended the throne under the title of Meiji (enlightened peace) to enact a series of drastic changes, including abolishing the shogunate, establishing a new constitution, and moving the capital to Edo, which was subsequently renamed Tokyo.[2]

Though he was more of a constitutional monarch than an actual ruler, Emperor Meiji quickly became an extremely potent unifying symbol while Japan's progressives desperately forced their country's development into a modernized nation. The era has since been called the Meiji Restoration, but the process was not easy, as there was a great deal of resistance, including civil war and lesser rebellions erupting in several parts of Japan. As a poor nation, Japan had to raise taxes and obtain loans to finance change, and even the established social structure had to be quickly remade. The result was nationally traumatic, amazingly fast, and spectacularly successful.

---

[2] Rickman 2003:44

Emperor Meiji

An all-out effort to remake Japan characterized this era. Hundreds of young men were sent abroad for education and to assess what foreign policies and practices would be helpful in developing Japan. The Japanese were interested in France's military, but after the French were crushed in the 1870 Franco-Prussian War, their interest turned to the German army and to British naval technology. They were also very interested in American technology, particularly in agriculture, which included bringing over many American advisors. Oddly enough, the most enduring result of the American advisers is the enduring Japanese passion for the American game of baseball.

Among other things, Japan set up 54,000 primary schools to develop literacy and inculcate modern Japanese nationalism. The Japanese were quite impressed with the utility of European and American university systems, and the 1886 Imperial University Ordinance explicitly stated that the institutions were to serve the interests of the state, which served to integrate higher education, nationalism and building the economy. In 1887, at the request of the military, Tokyo University added programs in arms technology and explosives, with the intent of producing military engineers, an innovation. Japan brought in experts in every technology, and its students abroad studied a very wide range of fields. Japanese entrepreneurs were remarkably successful, and Japan quickly began to industrialize. Technology and machinery were purchased and imported, and after the Japanese bought military equipment, they rapidly began to make their own. The Japanese navy at first bought warships built to order in Britain, but the Japanese quickly developed their own shipbuilding industry.

A major part of the Meiji Restoration was military modernization, and these changes had a profound effect on Japan as they completely upended the samurai order on both a macro and micro level. Contrary to popular belief, samurai had been influenced by Western military weapons and tactics well before the Meiji Restoration. Portuguese traders arrived in Japan as early as the 16th century, bringing Western weapons and techniques with them. These men were coveted by the samurai lords as they sought an advantage over their rivals on the island. With the help of the Portuguese traders, firearms and gunpowder were produced in secret on the island, revolutionizing warfare in Japan.[3] Vast armies of musket-wielding infantry engaged each other on the battlefields in Japan during the Warring States period, but firearm technology waned as the Tokugawa era progressed, at least until the arrival of Commodore Perry's American expedition.

The powerful guns on Perry's "black ships" seemed otherworldly to the feudal samurai, and the impact of such weapons left a profound effect on the shogun and daimyōs. The Tokugawa's rival clans saw these weapons as an opportunity to gain an advantage in ousting the Tokugawa shogun during the coming wars and defeating a possible foreign invasion. The Tokugawa shogunate also saw these firearms as a way to strengthen their political rule, which had weakened on the island.

By 1862, the Tokugawa government made a concentrated effort to organize and train its troops to meet the new Western standards, although troops were still drawn from the samurai class and not through conscription of the general population. 13,000 troops were trained over the next few years. The European military having the biggest effect on Japanese military reforms was the French, as at the time, the French army was considered the best in the world.[4] A military school was promptly established in Yokohama, an important port city for Japan, and around 250 handpicked students were sent to be trained under the French standard. The plan was to train an elite group of officers able to relocate to join the general army and disseminate their knowledge in person. As fate would have it, the rebellion against the Tokugawa shogun began before the training could spread through the shogun's armies, though individual soldiers were still able to utilize their training in command positions. This is demonstrated by men like Ōtori Keisuke, the rebel leader who "was an excellent strategist and maneuvered his men with the greatest ease. Most of the troops at his disposal had been drilled by Frenchmen, so that their good discipline and valor caused much trouble to the loyal forces."[5]

---

[3] Kublin 1949:24
[4] Kublin 1949:25
[5] Kublin 1949:25

Keisuke

A samurai with a katana in the 1860s

The Satsuma Rebellion was a huge test for the Meiji government's new military conscription and mobilization system. By the time the Great Saigō had been killed and the samurai's rebellion was crushed, the war was the costliest the Meiji army had fought to date. The end of the rebellion had violently eliminated any further prospects of an overthrow of the Meiji government, which managed to pass its first real test, bloodied but not defeated. The government would use the lessons from this war to strengthen the central army further.

All the while, the belief that the conscripts in the army lacked the discipline and fighting spirit of the samurai rebels continued to endure, even as their consistent victories over Saigō's rebels proved they were a potent fighting force. At least some individuals took note of this at the time, such as philosopher Nishi Amane, who praised the conscripts: "Although the rebels mocked government soldiers as 'peasant soldiers' [*hyakushōhei*], it was not so; [they] greatly surprised the rebels [lit. 'took the rebels' livers' (*ōi ni zokuto no tan o ubai*)]. It is said that even the conscripts among them revered their officers and protected them with their own bodies on occasion."[6]

For his part, Saigō has been lionized in Japan as the Great Saigō, and he still represents a unique kind of Japanese hero. He is praised not for any success, but because he pushed forward in his mission despite knowing that he wouldn't succeed.[7] Indeed, the entire rebellion has been romanticized, and the story has been told in countless dramatizations, most notably *The Last Samurai*, starring Tom Cruise, in 2003.[8] This romantic retelling of the rebellion paints the rebels as valiant defenders of the Japanese tradition and the Meiji government's army as a stale, faceless force. For instance, in an 1877 print by Adachi Ginko, government troops are shown as a uniform mass, hiding cowardly behind the safety of castle walls. The rebels, on the other hand, dominate the frame, and the leaders are identified by name.[9]

Although these cultural conceptions have had little influence on recent academic studies of the rebellion, they continue to influence the public's perception of the samurai. In reality, the samurai were soundly defeated, and the Meiji government's victory over the samurai rebels emphasized the inevitable transformation of the Japanese military in terms of technology, politics, and social change. The victory of the Meiji government in the Satsuma Rebellion solidified national conscription as the central army's future, and with the victory, the government had also succeeded in destroying the greatest threat to its military supremacy: the shizoku. These former samurai warriors had been defeated by conscripts,[10] and the demise of Saigō and his band of samurai rebels permanently finished off the Tokugawa-era military caste system and samurai caste privileges.

At the ground level, the rebellion also affected the central army's organizational culture. For many leaders, the defeat of the rebels represented the beginning stages of a modern Japanese army, and the fighting gave officers combat and tactical experience that would be channeled into reforms across the military in the 1880s. The response to the rebellion also functioned as a dress rehearsal for the army's ability to mobilize a large standing force ready to meet any threat, and this would have obvious ramifications over the next few decades of Japanese military expansion in Asia.

Despite the Meiji Restoration, the growing pains of the modernizing nation became apparent during a series of Korean civil disturbances in 1882 and 1884. Having sent advisors to Korea as

---

[6] Jaundrill 2016:147
[7] Yates 1994:450
[8] Jaundrill 2015:133
[9] Jaundrill 2016:133
[10] Jaundrill 2016:133

part of the 1876 treaty, Japan watched Korea experience its own pains of modernization. The rapid thrusting of Korea into international trade without the proper adaptations in industry and government led to urban inflation and rising resentment, both toward the royal court and foreign legations. In 1882, rioters attacked the Japanese delegation and the Korean Royal Court. It took an intervention by the Chinese Army to suppress the rioters and restore order, aptly demonstrating that despite Japan's grandstanding, China remained an influential force in Korea and Asia at large.

Japan's military failures in Korea and Taiwan, as well as China's defeat against France and other European powers, demonstrated to both the need to modernize and expand their militaries, including equipment, organization, and logistical coordination. Japan in particular looked to the lessons the West taught the Chinese, while the Chinese struggled to modernize while maintaining their dominant cultural identity in the region, a position slowly eroded by the French and British.

However, even as both Japan and China took a hard look at their roles in Asia following their entry into the greater world, they took very different courses of action. Japan, with a warrior class and firm footing as a modern, industrialized nation, looked to oppose Western encroachment and secure a more dominant role in Asia. For Japan, a secure future relied upon building up and keeping its military modernized.

In 1883, the conscription system was revised to reduce exemptions and incorporate a three level structure, sorted into three years of active service, four years in the first reserve, and five years in the second reserve. The ease for the wealthy to reduce their service time remained, however, and discontent festered due to the unequal nature of the army. What followed, despite later reform efforts in 1889, was an army of poor farmers' children led by the leftover elites of a society who looked down on their own soldiers with disdain.

China also attempted to adapt their military to the 19th century. However, the Chinese were so steeped in tradition that they refused to advance and reform on a united front in any sense, whether militarily, domestically, or politically. All of that would come back to haunt the Chinese when the Japanese made short work of the Chinese in the First Sino-Japanese War, and by being on the right side of World War I while China was racked by internal political divisions, Japan positioned itself for supremacy in Asia in the early 20th century.

Emperor Meiji was succeeded by his son, Emperor Yoshihito (posthumously known as Taishō), but the new emperor had several personal problems. He had mental issues, which led to an inability to articulate clearly, and he had eccentricities that prevented him from carrying out many of the normal ceremonial duties of the emperor. During one of his rare public appearances, at the opening of the Imperial Diet of Japan in 1913, he shocked and scandalized attendees by rolling up the paper on which his speech was printed and peering through the tube at the audience.

Taishō

After 1919, Emperor Yoshihito performed no further public duties and his role was supplanted by his son, Hirohito, who acted as regent while his father essentially became a recluse.

Despite the absence of the emperor, Japan continued to grow in power and prestige. During World War I, Japan allied with the Entente Powers and took the opportunity to seize some of Germany's possessions in Southeast Asia. It was also able to secure its position in Manchuria, though there was little actual conflict in the region during the war and Japan was little affected by the war, which devastated every powerful European nation.

After World War I, Japan joined the Big Four (America, Britain, France and Italy) at the peace negotiations and became one of only four permanent members in the League of Nations. However, all was not well in Japan. A series of Naval Conferences held under the auspices of the League of Nations in 1921-1922 sought to place limits on the naval power of the Great Nations, and a growing ultranationalist movement in Japan saw this as a deliberate attempt to reduce Japan's power in Southeast Asia. Then, in 1924, the United States passed the Johnson–Reed Act, also known as the Asian Exclusion Act, which severely limited Japanese immigration to America and classed Japanese in the same way as people from other Asian nations. Many Japanese were outraged at what they saw as a deliberate slight to Japanese prestige, and previously friendly relations between America and Japan were permanently soured.

Shortly after, in early December 1926, Emperor Yoshihito contracted pneumonia and died on December 25 at the Hayama Imperial Villa in Sagami Bay, south of Tokyo. He was succeeded by his son, the 25-five-year-old Prince Hirohito.

In many ways, Hirohito had been groomed for this. Prince Michinomiya Hirohito was born in on April 29, 1901 in the Aoyama Palace in Tokyo, the first grandson of the then reigning Emperor Meiji. His mother was Princess Kujō Sadako, a member of the Fujiwara, one of the highest-ranking court families with a history which stretched back to the late 12th century. His father, Crown Prince Yoshihito, was already chronically ill, and the birth of Hirohito was celebrated across Japan because it meant that the monarchy would continue uninterrupted even if his father proved unable to rule.

Hirohito in 1902

According to Japanese tradition, the infant Hirohito was raised not by his parents but by a surrogate family chosen by the emperor. Consequently, 70 days after his birth, Hirohito was sent to the care of the elderly Count Kawamura Sumiyoshi, a relation by marriage of Hirohito's mother. He was a retired vice admiral of the Japanese navy and a former Minster of the Navy in the Japanese Diet, but despite his military background, Count Sumiyoshi was a thoughtful and gentle man who schooled the young prince in Confucian principles. These principles stressed the need to be unselfish, heedful of the views of others, and persistence in the face of adversity. When Count Sumiyoshi died in 1904, Hirohito and his younger brother Chichibu returned to the royal household in Tokyo.

Hirohito's childhood could not have been easy. His father was already suffering from the mental confusion which would characterize his later life, and Hirohito's grandfather, the emperor, was a distant and rather stern figure. Hirohito's younger brother said of Emperor Meiji, "Never did I receive the warm, unqualified love that an ordinary grandfather gives to his grandchildren."[11] Although Hirohito never spoke of his grandfather with anything but respect, there is no reason to doubt that he was treated differently. Even his mother, Princess Kuj Sadako, was a fairly distant figure for much of his childhood.

In terms of his emotional development, one of the most important influences on the child was a young nurse, Adachi Taka, who spent a great deal of time with the prince and came to know him better than most. Taka would also go on to become the wife of Japanese Prime Minister Suzuki Kantarō, who held that position during the final months of World War II.

As this all indicates, life in the royal palace was stiff, formal, and carefully controlled in every respect. Hirohito and his brother often played war games, frequently reenacting scenes from the recent Russo-Japanese War, but the future emperor was never allowed to be defeated. Even while playing, it was felt that the future emperor must always succeed, so he was allowed to win whenever necessary. This reflected the authority of the autocratic Emperor Meiji. Draconian laws enacted in the late 19th century prohibited any adverse comments on the person of the emperor or his conduct. The Constitution of Japan allowed the government, the Imperial Diet, legislative power and a high degree of autonomy compared to other contemporary monarchies, but the emperor's will was expected to be taken into account, and all measures enacted by the Diet were subjected to a potential veto by the emperor. Education and the control of the military were specifically exempted from oversight by the Imperial Diet and placed under the direct authority of the emperor. This was the role which Hirohito was being groomed to fill, and everything he did was undertaken to prepare him for this.

In 1908, at the age of seven, Hirohito was enrolled in the Peers' School in Kyoto, opened in 1880 specifically to educate children of the imperial family and children from other noble families. The head of the school was General Nogi Maresuke, one of the victorious Japanese leaders during the Russo-Japanese War, and the general was charged by the emperor with the responsibility of ensuring that Hirohito received an appropriate education. The regimen would focus as much on physical development as academic attainment.

---

[11] Kawahara, *Tenno Hirohito no Showashi*, p. 30.

Nogi Maresuke

The death of Emperor Meiji in 1912 brought immediate and profound changes to Hirohito's life. As his troubled father became emperor, Hirohito became Crown Prince, heir to the throne. He was also given honorary ranks of Lieutenant in the Imperial Army and Ensign in the Imperial Navy.

From the beginning, the ascension of Hirohito's father to the throne of Japan posed a major problem for the country's political and military leaders. The laws and statutes enacted by Emperor Meiji gave the emperor a great deal of power, particularly in terms of control of the military, but the new emperor was frequently confused. In fact, it seemed he couldn't grasp military and naval matters in the slightest, and he was universally considered to be neglectful of his imperial duties. During a discussion about the selection of a new prime minister, Admiral Yamamoto Gonbee told a senior politician, "The emperor is not of the same caliber as the previous emperor. In my view it is loyal not to obey the emperor's word if we deem it to be disadvantageous to the state.[12]"

---

[12] Yasuda, *tenno no seijishi*, p. 159.

Most senior politicians and military leaders seemed to concur. With no formal constitutional change, the way in which Japan was governed changed virtually overnight, and Emperor Yoshihito was kept out of the public eye as far as possible. At the same time, this was not truly a coup - responsible leaders simply felt that the emperor could not be trusted to make rational decisions, so he was quietly excluded from the process of government. Throughout this time, there were hopes that his son, Hirohito, would make an altogether more effective emperor, and that his accession to the throne would bring about a reinstatement of the old ways.

As part of his grooming for the role of emperor and Supreme Commander of the Imperial Army and Navy, Hirohito was assigned a new mentor to replace General Nogi at the Peers' School. Hamao Arata, a former Minister of Education in the Imperial Diet, was given the role of Lord Steward of the Crown Prince and entrusted with the continuing education of Hirohito. Soon after, General Nogi and his wife committed ritual suicide.

Arata

At the age of 13, Hirohito moved on to the Togu-Ogakumonjo, a building constructed especially for his education within the grounds of the Takanawa Palace. For six years, Hirohito received an education that stressed the military, which meant that in addition to practical lessons on horsemanship, map-reading and gunnery, Hirohito was taught by some of Japan's most respected leaders on the practical and theoretical aspects of military strategy and tactics. Those responsible for Hirohito's were determined to produce an emperor who would be able to effectively fulfill his role as the country's supreme military leader.

This became even more important when Japan was shaken by a series of strikes and protests in the period following the end of World War I. Such events were virtually unknown in Japan, and the rice riots in Tokyo in 1918 became so threatening that Imperial Army troops were called upon to restore order. Violent strikes in a number of shipyards in 1921 brought a similar response. This in turn led to the army, which had previously been generally treated with near universal adulation, becoming unpopular with some segments of Japanese society. The country's leaders also blamed this unpopularity in part on the increasing invisibility of Emperor Yoshihito. The emperor's behavior had become so erratic and unpredictable that he had essentially disappeared from public life, and just at the time when a strong leader was needed to restore respect for the military, the emperor was unavailable. While the army had previously been seen (and had largely regarded itself) as an instrument of the emperor's will, it was now seen as the tool of an increasingly despotic government that utterly rejected calls for social and democratic reform.

Hirohito graduated from Togu-Ogakumonjo in May 1921, just before his 20th birthday, and he was as prepared as possible to take on the role of emperor, though some of his tutors expressed concern that he lacked the necessary aggressive martial spirit needed to lead the Imperial forces effectively.

By November 1921 it had become clear that the mental condition of the emperor had deteriorated to the point that something had to be done. On November 21, the emperor effectively retired and Hirohito was declared regent. From that time on, he began to undertake all the duties that would normally fall to the emperor.

Hirohito and his brothers in 1921

Hirohito and British Prime Minister David Lloyd George in 1921

A New Emperor

When Hirohito became regent, the Imperial Diet was quick to ensure that newspapers and other media in Japan carried the news that here at last was an acting emperor who was ready to carry out the full range of duties, especially in terms of commanding the armed forces. Hirohito was frequently pictured in uniform, taking part in army training exercises, reviewing troops, and visiting warships.

A strong leader was needed more than ever before because of divisions appearing at every level of Japanese society. The strikes and protests following the end of World War I had led to a reduction in the respect most Japanese had previously afforded their leaders, and this extended to the army, now viewed by many as an instrument used by the government to keep the people in check. Even within the ruling classes there were deep and seemingly irreconcilable differences.

One of the major issues was the series of arms limitation treaties culminating in the Washington Naval Treaty, which Japan had signed. These placed limits on the naval power of signatories, and for Japan, this was a significant issue. Japan's expansion into Korea and Manchuria had produced new resources, but many Japanese political and military leaders wanted to see their country's influence spread even further across Southeast Asia.

Even in the early 1920s, many Japanese leaders recognized that expansion in the Pacific would almost certainly bring Japan into conflict with the United States, and such a conflict would be decided almost entirely by naval power. Thus, a strong Japanese navy was an essential element of the aims of expansionists, but under the terms of the treaty, Japan was allowed to build only three capital ships for every five that America created. The moderate faction within the Japanese leadership was willing to agree to this, even though it meant abandoning plans for expansion. Appeasement of America, they argued, was essential because Japan could not hope to match the industrial capacity of the United States and would inevitably lose any conflict. Set against this was a right-wing group which supported the policy of aggressive expansion and accepted the possibility of conflict with the Americans; indeed, some even seemed to welcome this prospect. These officials believed that while Japanese naval forces might be outnumbered, the superior quality of their ships and crews would allow them to defeat America. Hirohito found himself caught between these two groups on the right and the left.

In September 1923, Japan suffered a catastrophe which briefly deflected attention from politics. A devastating earthquake struck Tokyo and the port of Yokohama and caused extensive damage across the whole Kantō region. Over 100,000 people were killed, and more than 40,000 simply disappeared and were presumed to have died. Half a million homes were destroyed in Tokyo alone.

This was the worst natural disaster to afflict Japan in the 20th century, but in its wake came even more disturbing events. A false rumor spread that Koreans living in Japan were taking advantage of the earthquake to loot businesses, and some newspapers even carried stories that Koreans were poisoning wells in areas in Tokyo and Yokohama. In response, mobs of enraged Japanese began to murder Koreans or anyone they thought might be Korean. Up to 10,000 Koreans were killed, as were an estimated 1,000 Chinese mistakenly believed to be Korean.

This sort of mob violence had not been seen before in Japan, and this illustrated even more clearly the way in which Japanese society was fragmenting. In several cases, police officers or soldiers participated in the killings or handed Koreans over to mobs who subsequently murdered them. The army and police, who largely supported the right-wing activists, also took advantage of the chaos following the earthquake to abduct and murder a number of socialist and anarchist political leaders. They later justified this by claiming that they believed these activists might take advantage of social unrest to foment revolution, though there is no evidence to support the claims.

Even within the Japanese army itself, there were incidents of insubordination and even outright mutiny. In 1921, Minister of the Army Tanaka Giichi warned that obedience in the lower ranks of the army could no longer be taken for granted: "[I]n recent years they have become bold and rebellious in their attitudes, and criminal acts have increased, especially cases where men form small groups and act violently."[13]

The disintegration of what had been, up to the end of the First World War, a stable and peaceful society was underlined even further in December 1923 when the unthinkable happened. Hirohito was traveling to deliver his inaugural address to the Imperial Diet on December 27 when shots were fired at his carriage. One bullet shattered a window of the carriage, but Hirohito was unhurt. A young anarchist, Daisuke Nanba, was arrested, tried and quickly executed. At the trial, he railed against "unjust institutions" and made it clear that he supported the Bolshevik Revolution in the Soviet Union. Many on the extreme right took this as a further reason to clamp down not just on political activists, but also on newspapers and magazines that supported liberal and radical movements.

When Hirohito married Princess Nagako in January 1924, the ceremony was deliberately kept relatively low-key. It was justifiably believed that a lavish event would cause even more popular unrest, especially given that large parts of the capital still lay in ruins following the earthquake. A year later, the couple celebrated the birth of their first child, and a year after that, in December 1926, Emperor Yoshihito died. On Christmas Day, Hirohito became the 124th emperor of Japan. Given that he had been acting as regent on his father's behalf for several years, this did not bring major changes to Hirohito's life, but it did finally install him formally in Japanese military and political life.

---

[13] Fujiwara, *Showa tenno no jogonen senso*, p. 42.

Hirohito and his wife

As it turned out, Hirohito's ascension to power coincided with the start of the greatest period of upheaval Japan ever experienced.

The Rise of Militarism

Hirohito on the Imperial stallion Shirayuki

As Hirohito became emperor, a new law had just been passed in Japan which gave the vote to virtually all Japanese males. This was a significant change, and it led to an increase in interest in political parties amongst peasants and lower classes, which inadvertently brought a period of virtual anarchy as these parties vied to control the country.

The militarists and their supporters reacted to the extension of voting rights and the increase of socialist and peasant parties with horror. It was clear that the new parties had little respect for the army or for the emperor, and many did not accept that the emperor had a divine right to rule. The growing left-wing movement was given additional impetus when a financial crisis struck Japan in 1927, increasing unemployment and causing some banks to fail. In part, the crisis could be traced back to bad debts incurred during the earthquake in 1923, but there was also plenty of evidence of mismanagement, and this sparked a financial panic which lasted until the summer of 1927.

During the financial crisis, a new prime minister was appointed in the form of Baron Tanaka Giichi, a retired general and leading member of the conservative *Seiyūkai* political party. Tanaka used mass arrests and detentions without trial to limit the growing power of communist and socialist parties. Traditionally, the Seiyūkai had close links with and was supported by the Japanese army, but events in Manchuria destabilized Tanaka's position in 1928.

Tanaka

Within the Japanese army, there were a number of ultranationalist secret societies dedicated to crushing the left-wing political movement and expanding Japanese power through military action. These were particularly prevalent within the Kwantung Army, the Japanese army of occupation in Manchuria, which operated as a virtually autonomous force. On June 4, 1928, a bomb planted by officers of the Kwantung Army killed Zhang Zuolin, the military dictator of the Republic of China. The Kwantung Army had become infuriated by Zuolin's failure to defeat the National Revolutionary Army, and when Prime Minister Tanaka demanded that the officers responsible be publicly court-martialed, the army refused and the incident was kept secret. Without the support of the army, the position of Tanaka was precarious, and when Hirohito sided with the army and openly criticized him, Tanaka and his cabinet resigned en masse in July 1929.

Tanaka was replaced by Hamaguchi Osachi, a leading member of the main opposition to the Seiyūkai Party, the moderate and anti-militaristic *Minseitō* Party.

Hamaguchi Osachi

Hamaguchi focused on the Japanese economy, which had never entirely recovered from the crisis of 1927. Amongst other measures, he encouraged exports and aligned the yen to the Gold Standard. He combined these with austerity measures, including reduced spending on the army and navy, and he signed yet another treaty which limited Japan's ability to build warships: the London Naval Treaty of 1930. Nothing that he did seemed to help, and the Japanese economy entered another depression in early 1930.

In November 1930, Hamaguchi was shot and grievously wounded by Tomeo Sagoya, a member of the *Aikokusha*, another right-wing, ultranationalist secret society. Hamaguchi survived, but he never fully recovered from his injuries. He died in August 1931.

During 1931, it became apparent that elements of the Japanese army were out of control. In the Wanpaoshan Incident, Chinese farmers supported by Chinese police clashed with Korean farmers backed by Japanese police in Wanpaoshan, Manchuria. The Koreans won, but ensuing violence in Korea subsequently left more than 100 Chinese residents dead, and in In June of that year, Chinese troops killed IJA Captain Shintarō Nakamura and his companions in Manchuria, assuming them to be spies. The military tried to turn the Nakamuro Incident into an excuse for action, but by sensing the danger, the Chinese vigorously pursued Nakamuro's killers and deprived the Kwantung Army of yet another potentially promising opportunity to start a war.

Shintarō Nakamura and Entarō Isugi

Nevertheless, a general refusal by the Chinese to cooperate ultimately provided the Japanese with a solid pretext led to the Mukden Incident. Historians remain divided on real responsibility for the action. Some hold that the civilian government of Japan did not desire the outbreak of hostilities, and that the Kwantung Army acted independently, taking advantage of its distance from civilian authorities in the home islands to manufacture an incident against the Cabinet's and Emperor's wishes. Others acknowledge that the Kwantung Army took the initiative, but they believe the government dithered and looked the other way deliberately to give the military the opportunity to execute a plan whose benefits the Japanese government could reap if successful and deny should it fail. Yet others aver that Tokyo gave secret orders to the Kwantung officers who carried out the plan, moved by a largely unified desire to seize Manchuria among both civilian and Army authorities. Given the willingness of Japanese soldiers and officers to take responsibility and punishment (even execution) upon themselves to spare the Emperor even a hint of opprobrium, this latter theory remains possible.

Regardless of whatever machinations took place behind the scenes, two men, Lieutenant

Colonel Ishiwara Kanji and Colonel Itagaki Seishiro, headed the actual plotters in Mukden. Ishiwara, a Nichiren Buddhist with a shaved head, and Itagaki, a mustached career officer hanged for war crimes after World War II, planned a false flag attack against the South Manchurian Railway for late September 1931. The timing coincided with the end of the harvest of sorghum or great millet, whose 10-foot stalks might otherwise interfere with rapid infantry marches across country.

Ishiwara

Itagaki

   The Emperor and Army High Command dispatched Major General Tatekawa Yoshitsugu to Manchuria in September, ostensibly to bring the Kwantung Army back in check. Rather suspiciously, the outspoken opinions of Tatekawa ensured that everyone in the Japanese government already knew that he supported a military annexation of Manchuria, the exact event the government, army, and Emperor allegedly ordered him to prevent. Even more suspect, his commission called on him to meet specifically with the two leading Kwantung plotters, Ishiwara and Itagaki.

Yoshitsugu

When Tatekawa arrived on September 18th, 1931, Itagaki met him, accompanying him on the train into Mukden from a point several hours outside the city. Emperor Hirohito had once described Itagaki as the "stupidest man alive," but he possessed notable social skills and carried out his role to perfection.

The "good inn" proved to be the Kikubumi, a Japanese geisha inn in Mukden. There, Tatekawa ate a superb dinner, drank quantities of alcohol, and, at 9:00 p.m. sharp, retired to his room with an attractive young geisha. In the meantime, a detachment of Japanese soldiers traversed the South Manchurian Railway line on handcars, disembarking at a point fairly close to the Peitaying Barracks, occupied by between 7,000 and 10,000 Chinese soldiers.

The Japanese soldiers placed dynamite charges near the rail line, setting them off to produce a thunderous explosion at 10:00 p.m. They then fired their rifles into the air in wild volleys to simulate a brief firefight. Though the Japanese later claimed the Chinese dynamited the tracks, destroying several yards, a scheduled passenger train coming south from Changchun hurtled through at 10:30 p.m. at top speed. Had a gap existed, derailment would have been unavoidable. However, the passengers later reported that they did not even feel a bump during the trip. The Japanese sappers had, in fact, deliberately detonated the dynamite a safe distance from the rails, inflicting no damage. Some of the plotters had suggested actually blowing up the train with a bomb, in the manner of Zhang Zuolin's assassination. More senior schemers disallowed this, not wishing to kill Japanese passengers – or be later charged with their murder if the truth emerged.

The tragic farce grew more transparent as it developed. Ishiwara's men deposited three freshly killed Chinese in uniform – possibly soldiers kidnapped earlier, or even a trio of luckless peasants dressed in military garb, then executed in cold blood – next to the undamaged railway tracks as "saboteurs shot while escaping." The Japanese pointed the heads of all three corpses towards the distant Peitaying Barracks in case anyone failed to understand the glaringly obvious scenario already constructed.

Two Russian 9.5 inch naval guns, brought into the town by the conspirators and based in a concrete battery built as a "swimming pool" earlier in the summer, opened fire on the Chinese barracks at 11:00 p.m. Not even bothering with the pretense of an investigation, the Japanese mustered their troops to attack the barracks, killing the guards, whose officers had equipped them only with dummy rifles due to their untrained state. Major General Tategawa slipped from the arms of his geisha and out the back door of the inn to join this force, though the geisha later swore he spent the entire night with her.

Meanwhile, Ishiwara reported to Lieutenant General Shigeru Honjō in Port Arthur, then taking a bath, to report on the situation. Though the Japanese initiated aggression against the Chinese, Ishiwara carefully cast his report to depict the opposite: "The odds against us are staggering. The entire countryside may rise. Offense is our only defense. I hope, sir, that you will allow Itagaki to proceed with the contingency plan that has already been prepared."

Honjō

Honjō made a great show of berating Itagaki over the telephone, but soon came to the actual point of the call: giving him permission to attack Mukden itself at 11:30 p.m.

The transparency of the Mukden Incident could hardly have increased; the Kwantung Army created a scenario in which an explosion in the darkness near a rail line at 10:00 p.m. could be ascribed so confidently to a secret Chinese plot that it justified an attack on the city just 90 minutes later – surely one of the most rapid forensic successes in history at a scene of random terrorism. Even Uchida Yasuya, the Japanese president of the South Manchurian Railway Company, deemed the situation a false flag attack: "The reason for military occupation is reportedly the destruction of the railway by Chinese troops from the North Barracks, but railway supervisors have been sent to the spot three times so far and have been refused entry […] The present military action has been practiced as an emergency exercise since the 14th […] and is assumed to be the execution of a prearranged plan."

While the Japanese used that pretext to invade and hold the rest of Manchuria, in December 1931 a new Japanese prime minister was appointed. Prime Minister Inukai Tsuyoshi, a moderate who was opposed to Japanese military expansion in Manchuria and who demanded the right to send a representative of the government to Manchuria to halt any other military activity, wanted to negotiate with the Chinese. As a result, there was an attempted coup in May 1932 by young naval officers supported by army cadets. 11 young naval officers went to the official residence of the prime minister and murdered Inukai Tsuyoshi. Assassins also intended to kill Charlie Chaplin, who was at that time visiting Japan, in the hope that this would provoke an immediate war with the United States. The attempt to kill Chaplin and the coup failed, but the assassination of yet another Japanese politician marked the effective end of any semblance of democracy in Japan and the beginning of the rise of the militarists to absolute power.

Inukai Tsuyoshi

Kwantung Army operations in Manchuria continued without government permission, sanction, or approval. The Kwantung Army quickly conquered large areas of Manchuria and brought them under direct Japanese control. The war in Manchuria was supported by most of the Japanese people, not least because it was portrayed as a means of ending the economic depression that was still affecting the whole country. With seemingly easy victories and overwhelming public support, the government decided to support operations in Manchuria and sent another three infantry divisions to the area to support the Kwantung Army.

Part of the issue for successive Japanese governments was that the constitution made it a requirement that both the army and navy were represented in cabinets. This meant that without the support of the military, no government could survive for long. As the military was generally dominated by hard-line militarists who supported aggressive expansion, the Japanese government was locked into a policy of supporting military operations even when they were undertaken without orders.

All the while, the operations by Japanese forces in Manchuria were widely reported outside Japan and were generally condemned, especially the indiscriminate bombing of civilians and the generally brutal behavior of army members towards prisoners of war. Japan became internationally isolated and faced increasing hostility from the United States and other Western nations, including Britain, the Netherlands, and France, which had colonies in Southeast Asia. President Herbert Hoover refused to recognize the puppet state of Manchukuo in Manchuria, and Hoover sent a formal diplomatic note to Japan stating that the United States would not recognize any new state in the region created as a result of force by Japan.

During this time, the emperor was generally supportive of the army and the extreme right-wing of Japanese politics. In January 1932, Emperor Hirohito published a formal imperial communication which praised the actions of the Kwantung Army, declared their actions to be "self defense," and even declared that the Kwantung Army had increased "the authority of the emperor's army." This statement was widely promulgated throughout Japan, and the obvious support of the emperor for the actions of the army in Manchuria made it even more difficult for moderate politicians to speak out. Now, denouncing the actions of the Kwantung Army could be seen as a direct challenge to the will of the emperor.

The senior members of the Kwantung Army were not punished for acting without orders from the government. Instead, Hirohito offered a large number of awards and advancements to members of the army for their service in Manchuria. This further strengthened the view that the emperor supported aggressive expansion through military action.

Emperor Hirohito survived another assassination attempt in January 1932 when a Korean independence supporter hurled a hand grenade at the emperor's carriage. However, of even more concern to the emperor was the League of Nations' Lytton Report into Japanese actions in Manchuria, which formally stated that the League would not accept any change in the status of Manchuria resulting from Japanese aggression. The Kwantung Army reacted in February 1933 by mounting its largest operation to date, with more than 20,000 Japanese troops advancing into the Jehol area of Manchuria. They met little effective resistance and quickly brought the new region under their control.

International reaction was swift and negative. At the League of Nations, the Japanese claim that they were simply reacting to provocations from Chinese forces was not accepted. In March 1933, Japan formally withdrew from the League of Nations, further increasing its isolation in international affairs. However, the economic depression which was affecting the United States and many European nations, as well as the rise of the Nazis in Germany, meant that no country was willing to take direct military action to stop Japanese expansion in Manchuria.

Manchuria was also becoming increasingly important to Japan. The raw materials from this area were essential for maintaining Japanese industrial output, and international isolation meant Japan might face a future in which it would not be able to import such materials from elsewhere. The maintenance of Manchuria under Japanese control therefore became a strategic imperative for the burgeoning empire.

The Kwantung Army continued to act as an independent force. In April 1933, it attacked Chinese territory in the vicinity of Beijing, but was forced to withdraw. In May, another more successful attack was mounted in North China. Neither action had been ordered or sanctioned by the military, and privately, Hirohito expressed his concerns that the Kwantung Army seemed to be operating "independent of the supreme command." Publicly, however, he continued to support all elements of the Japanese army and navy and rewarded members of the Kwantung Army.

Towards the end of 1933, a documentary film was produced by the Osaka *Mainichi* newspaper. *Japan in the National Emergency* was an attempt to justify Japanese action in Manchuria and was produced with the support of the Army Ministry. This documentary was extremely well received in Japan, not least because it seemed to suggest that the actions of the army in Manchuria were being carried out in accordance with the will of the emperor. The documentary featured commentary by Army Minister Baron Sadao Araki, who noted at one point, "The spirit of the Japanese military manifests the sacred spirit of his majesty who commands the Japanese military. I believe our spirit expresses the emperor's heart, which is why the imperial forces move only at the emperor's command."

This was a very important point for the audience, many of whom still believed in the divine status of the emperor. From what is known of the actions of the Kwantung Army in Manchuria, it also seems to be manifestly untrue, because on more than one occasion Hirohito only learned of the army's plans after it already began offensive operations. Far from acting on the command of the emperor; the emperor was being forced to legitimize the actions of the army after the fact. However, any doubts Hirohito may have had remained unspoken, and he never openly condemned the army for its actions in Manchuria or elsewhere. As a result, most people inside Japan and elsewhere believed the army account, which was that they were acting in accordance with the will of the emperor.

From 1934-1936, the belief that the army was carrying out the orders of the emperor became fused with a claim that Japanese expansion was a benevolent act, introducing the wisdom of the emperor to other people and ensuring that they lived in peace and harmony. This was widely accepted in Japan, but the brutal truth of what was happening in Manchuria was viewed very differently in other countries. Within the Japanese army, there was also a struggle between the few remaining moderates and the radical *Kōdōha* (Imperial Way) faction, which sought to use the supposed support of the emperor as a justification for the replacement of the democratic government in Japan with a military dictatorship. This came to a head when General Tetsuzan Nagata, a leading moderate in the military and a member of the Ministry of War, was killed by Lt. Col. Saburo Aizawa, a supporter of *Kōdōha,* who burst into Nagata's office and stabbed the general with a samurai sword.

The trial of Saburo began in January 1936, but while it was still in progress, an army mutiny led by officers who supported *Kōdōha* erupted in Tokyo on February 26. The mutineers assassinated several prominent moderates, including Lord Keeper of the Privy Seal Saito Makoto and the Finance Minister Takahashi. It seems that Hirohito was concerned that the mutineers, who had a great deal of support within the military, were planning to force him to abdicate in favor of his younger brother, who had shown some sympathy for the *Kōdōha* faction. For once the emperor acted quickly and demanded that the mutiny should be quelled before the rebel force, which numbered about 1,000, could march on the Royal Palace.

On February 27 Hirohito declared martial law in Tokyo, and within two days the leaders of the mutiny were under arrest and the threat to the emperor was removed. The ringleaders were tried in secret and executed in April. For many outside observers, Hirohito's swift and decisive response to the mutiny was seen as confirmation that he supported the action of the army in Manchuria. After all, he had barely responded at all when the Kwantung Army seemed to act without official sanction, whereas his swift quelling of the mutiny in Tokyo indicated that he had the power and authority to act when he felt this was necessary. In retrospect, some historians have chosen to interpret this as showing that Hirohito was prepared to take decisive action only when his own position and safety were threatened.

It was certainly notable that in 1937, when a series of small-scale conflicts in Manchuria erupted into full-scale war between Japan and the Republic of China (ROC), the emperor had little to say even when the Japanese military committed the most bestial acts of cruelty on the Chinese civilian population. That July, Japanese forces began a full-scale invasion of territory controlled by the Chinese, beginning with an attack on the city of Shanghai. The battle for Shanghai lasted for three months and caused up to 300,000 casualties. It was quickly followed by an attack on Nanking, which caused international outrage and the further isolation of Japan. Nonetheless, Japanese forces captured Nanking on December 13, and for a period of at least three weeks, Japanese soldiers massacred prisoners of war and Chinese civilians. No one is entirely certain how many died in the massacre, but some estimates suggest as many as 300,000 unarmed people were killed.

Within Japan, public opinion seemed to be largely indifferent to this slaughter. In January 1937, the *Tokyo Nichi Nichi Shimbun* newspaper enthusiastically covered a contest between two

Japanese officers to be the first to kill 100 people with a sword. Outside Japan, the response to what became known as the Rape of Nanking was generally one of horror and condemnation. The atrocities were covered by a number of newspapers, and the failure of the Japanese emperor to make any public statement on the conduct of the military in Nanking reinforced the view that he understood what was being done and supported it. As such, people in Japan and elsewhere believed that the brutal actions were carried out in accordance with the will of the emperor.

The string of virtually uninterrupted Japanese victories in China came to an end in 1938. Even with the introduction of higher budgets for military spending, full national mobilization, and the use of banned chemical weapons, the vast area of Manchuria was beyond the capacity of the Japanese military to control effectively. Around October 1938, the Japanese position switched to strategic defense, with all available troops being required just to hang on to the territory conquered since 1936.

In May 1939, the Kwantung Army was faced with another threat when elements of the Japanese army became involved in fighting with units of the Soviet Red Army on the border between Manchukuo and Mongolia. This undeclared war continued for months, inflicting almost 20,000 Japanese casualties until a truce was finally agreed to in September 1939. By that time, World War II had started in Europe.

In 1936, Japan had signed the Anti-Comintern Pact, thus forming an alliance with Nazi Germany. A year later, Hirohito's brother, Prince Chichibu, attended the Nuremberg Rally and had personal meetings with Adolf Hitler. Japan was concerned at the prospect of conflict with the Soviet Union in Manchuria and Mongolia, and this alliance with Germany was seen as a way of negating the Soviet threat.

However, a more significant threat to Japan was the increasingly hostile attitude of the Roosevelt administration in America. For many years, America had pursued a policy of appeasement, but events such as the Rape of Nanking had hardened public opinion in the United States against Japan. In July 1939, Roosevelt's administration gave notice that it did not intend to renew the US-Japanese Treaty of Commerce and Navigation, which would lapse in January 1940.

This was potentially a major blow to Japan, because without imports from America of oil and raw materials for industry, Japan's ability to continue to wage war in China would be threatened. America's continuing protests about Japanese aggression in China had been ignored by military and political leaders for several years, and this should not have come as a surprise. Even an irritated Hirohito was moved to comment on the failure of Japanese leaders to anticipate this. He complained, "Unless we reduce the size of our army and navy by one-third, we won't make it. They should have prepared for something like this a long time ago. It's unacceptable for them to be making a commotion about it now."

On August 23, 1939, Japanese politicians were stunned to discover that Hitler had signed a non-aggression pact with the Soviet Union. This was in direct contravention of the alliance which already existed with Japan, and within two weeks the reason for the pact became obvious when German troops attacked Poland from the west. A short time later, Red Army units attacked from the east. Britain and France declared war on Germany a few days later, and with those moves, World War II had begun.

Many leaders in Japan were very concerned about the reaction of America, and some feared that the United States would immediately join the Allies. Hirohito was instrumental in keeping Japan out of the war at this time, insisting that the army remained focused on winning the war in Manchuria and resisting calls for a closer alliance with Germany against the Allies.

In April and May 1940, German forces rolled west in Europe, rapidly conquering Norway and Denmark, and then Luxembourg, Belgium, the Netherlands, and France. By the end of June 1940, Britain was the only European nation still actively opposing Nazi Germany.

Japan Enters World War II

For Japan, the collapse of European countries which had colonies in Southeast Asia presented a new and unexpected opportunity. France and the Netherlands both controlled territory in Asia, as did Britain, which many assumed would be forced to capitulate to Germany by the end of the year. If Japan could seize these colonies, this would provide some of the oil and raw materials needed by Japanese industry that had previously come from America.

In July 1940, at a secret government and military liaison conference, it was agreed that Japanese forces should occupy French Indochina and the Dutch East Indies, and possibly also British Malaya. It was hoped that it would only be necessary to fight Britain for possession of these territories, and those in favor noted that British armed forces were fully committed to defending the homeland against a potential Nazi invasion. The only major opposition to such a move might come from America, something that was recognized at the conference.

Hirohito did not attend the conference, but he formally approved its conclusions. In September 1940, the emperor issued Imperial Headquarters Army Order Number 458, which ordered the army to begin preparations for an invasion of French Indochina. Later the same month, Japan signed the Tripartite Pact, a closer alliance with Nazi Germany and Italy that recognized Japan's right to expand and dominate in East Asia. An Imperial Rescript issued soon after under the emperor's name noted, "As the disasters that humankind may suffer are immeasurable, we sincerely hope to bring about a cessation of hostilities and a restoration of peace, and have therefore ordered the government to ally with Germany and Italy, nations which share the same intentions as ourselves." Of course, the rescript failed to mention that the "restoration of peace" was to be achieved through military conquest, and that it risked conflict with America.

As Japan moved inexorably towards war, Hirohito ensured that he was a central part of the decision-making apparatus of the Japanese military. He began to send aides, including his brothers, on inspection tours of military facilities, and they brought back to him detailed reports. He also began to watch foreign newsreels and read foreign newspapers.

By the spring of 1941, Japanese politicians had become aware that the German-Soviet non-aggression pact signed in 1939 was a sham designed purely to allow Germany to invade Poland without Russian intervention. By early June, the Japanese were aware that Hitler intended to begin an invasion of the Soviet Union later that summer, and in July, a document prepared by a secret imperial conference and approved by the emperor noted that it might soon be necessary to go to war with Britain and the Soviet Union, and that this might in turn provoke war with America. This document also mentioned the creation of a "Greater East Asia Co-prosperity Sphere," a euphemism for new territory which was to be conquered by Japan.

On July 28, 1941, over 40,000 Japanese troops occupied French Indochina, though this was achieved peacefully after negotiations with the conquered Vichy French government. President Roosevelt reacted by freezing all Japanese assets in America and placing a complete embargo on the export of oil to Japan. This was a major blow to Japanese expansion plans, as they needed oil for their ships, tanks, and aircraft.

At the same time, Roosevelt and the military planned accordingly for a Japanese attack in 1941, and one of the most obvious targets for potential Japanese expansion was the Philippines, an imperial possession still held by American forces. With a careful eye on Japan's expansion, the United States moved to protect the Philippines, which also induced President Roosevelt to station a majority of the Pacific fleet at Pearl Harbor.

Assuming that aggression toward British targets and the Dutch East Indies would bring the United States into the war, a faction within the Japanese military leadership headed by Naval Chief of Staff Admiral Osami Nagano came to believe that a quick, pre-emptive war against America was the only solution. Otherwise, if Japan delayed too long, they would not have sufficient oil reserves to fight effectively.

Nagano

By 1941, the Japanese navy was one of the most capable in the world and so formidable that it was equaled only by the American and British navies. At that point, however, both of those nations were heavily committed in the Atlantic and Mediterranean respectively. Japan's navy was a well balanced and modern force, building on a recent but highly successful naval tradition. Japan had only emerged from relative isolation during the 19th century, but as an island nation it had a cultural affinity for the sea and a strategic appreciation of its importance. In fact, Japan had unashamedly turned to the world's premier naval power for advice on modern naval thinking. In 1912, the Russo-Japanese war, which had stagnated on the ground at Port Arthur, was decisively resolved in Japan's favor by means of the massive sea battle of Tsushima. The Japanese had used modern British-built ships with British advisors onboard to smash the antiquated Tsarist fleet. With that, Japan had arrived as a naval power.

It has often been pointed out that the American carriers' absence from Pearl Harbor ultimately spelled Japan's doom, but the attack on Pearl Harbor was heavily focused on hitting the battleships that Japan perceived as the key index of naval power. This was all straight out of Mahan's textbook, but the Japanese would learn in 1942 at Midway that Mahan's strategies were befitting of an earlier era. Notwithstanding this mixed doctrine, Japan had a well-balanced, well-trained, experienced[14] and modern fleet with which to confront America and the Allies. What she did not have was the resource base necessary to conduct extended operations.

Japan's *Yamato*, the biggest battleship in the world in 1941

While the U.S. went about expanding its navy, the military went about putting plans in place to confront Japan in the Pacific. Plan Orange specifically addressed a possible war with Japan and had been evolving since before World War I.[15] It envisaged a strategic withdrawal to San Diego, while the U.S. Navy could be built up and strengthened, followed by a progressive counter-offensive. This was conservative but also realistic. It assumed short-term Japanese superiority and accepted that the Hawaiian Islands and Philippines would have to hang on - and possibly face invasion - in the absence of the main battle fleet. These were not concessions that were easy to make politically, and General Douglas MacArthur would vocally make the case for a stronger, more proper defense of the Philippines.

While that step was not forthcoming, Roosevelt did have the main Pacific fleet sent to Pearl Harbor, where it was meant as a deterrent to let Japan know the U.S. meant business. At the same time, however, stationing the Pacific fleet at Pearl Harbor meant the U.S. was potentially

---

[14] Japanese naval units, including her carriers, had been integral to her war effort in China.
[15] And its successor "Rainbow 5" factoring in British participation, followed by the "Plan Dog" memorandum and Roosevelt's "Europe First" policy, during early 1942.

leaving the Philippines exposed, and American military planners were constantly in fear of a Japanese attack there in late 1941.

What is clear is that by stationing the Pacific fleet at Pearl Harbor, the U.S. did not have the ability to seriously contest a Japanese incursion into the Southern Resource Area in 1941. In other words, the U.S. could not actively prevent Japanese attacks against British Malaya or the Dutch East Indies. The decision to station the navy in Hawaii might very well have also signaled that Roosevelt had no intention of seriously contesting such an attack either. Thus, just what action Roosevelt would have taken in response to a Japanese attack on British Malaya or the Dutch East Indies without a corresponding attack on Pearl Harbor or the Philippines remains an unanswerable mystery.

As a result of these decisions, there was a marked asymmetry in both perceptions and capabilities as Japan and the U.S. stared each other down from across the Pacific in mid-1941. The U.S. was not ready for a Pacific war and did not want war at all, and though it was making preparations it was in no position politically or militarily to jump to the defense of the European empires in Asia. At the same time, the oil embargo indicated they were not going to underwrite Japan's aggression against China either. Without those resources, and operating under the potentially mistaken belief that aggression against Allied possessions would draw the U.S. into the war, Japan came to view the U.S. as the key obstacle to its ambitions. Both sides recognized that Japan had at least a temporary naval supremacy in 1941, and to Japan's High Command this gave them what they viewed as a small window during which to deliver a decisive blow that might secure a permanent advantage.

For his part, Hirohito appeared to agree with Nagano. His only reservation was whether Japan could actually defeat the United States, not the morality of further aggressive expansion. Finally, on November 5, 1941, an important decision was taken: "Our policy toward the United States, Britain, and the Netherlands was decided upon at the imperial conference that convened in the emperor's presence at 10:30 A.M." Negotiations with America aimed at easing sanctions continued, but from that time on, it was agreed that the Japanese navy would undertake an attack on the fleet at Pearl Harbor. No direct evidence has been found to confirm that the emperor supported this approach, but there is no evidence that he disapproved, and his disapproval would almost certainly have meant a change of course for Japan.

Though the attack in December 1941 came as a great surprise and is still considered a daring strategy over 70 years later, such an attack had been contemplated by Japanese military officials as early as 1927, and in 1928 Captain Isoroku Yamamoto had proposed such an attack in a lecture he gave at the Navy Torpedo School. During the 1930s, as Japan built up its navy and expanded across Asia, the concept of a strike against the U.S. Pacific Fleet gained momentum, and the Japanese had gamed such an attack on a number of occasions. What they had concluded was that they could expect heavy casualties, particularly if the Americans detected the Japanese fleet as it moved into position, and they were also worried about their ability to destroy battleships in harbor due to the difficulties of running torpedoes in shallow water. In overcoming that seeming disadvantage, they were inadvertently aided by Britain following her successful strike against the Italian navy at Taranto, which relied exclusively on airpower. That would in turn shift Japan's strategy, which would rely on planes to deliver the devastating surprise.

Yamamoto

When the Japanese High Command took the momentous decision to plan in earnest for a surprise attack on the American base at Pearl Harbor, it was with a view to delivering this psychological and political shock. In other words, Japan intended to deliver a message to the American people, not the American military. There was nothing new to this strategy so far as Japan was concerned - Japan's military doctrine emphasized the "will to fight" at all levels, and it had previously begun a war against Russia with a surprise assault at Port Arthur.

On November 26, as the Japanese fleet was planning to set sail toward Pearl Harbor, the Roosevelt administration gave a document to the Japanese ambassador that consisted of two parts, one an oral statement and one an outline of a proposed basis for agreement between the United States and Japan. Japan's leaders had already chosen war by the time the ambassador received that document, but the ambassador himself was in the dark regarding the impending attack on Pearl Harbor. Japan's ambassador was Kurusu Saburo, and he was assisted by diplomat Nomura Kichisaburo. Together they were instructed to settle the issue by the end of November 1941, so they continued to unwittingly negotiate the terms of a peace that never had a chance, hoping against hope that they could stave off war.

As both sides feebly negotiated the wide gaps between them, the Japanese fleet continued heading toward Hawaii while operating under radio silence. This was critical because unbeknownst to the Japanese, the Allies' codebreakers were able to decrypt their communications long before Pearl Harbor. And though Japan was unaware that they had successfully broken the Japanese encryptions on their diplomatic communications, they assumed the U.S. would be monitoring their naval communications in the Pacific and thus had their radio operators sending out fake radio communications, fooling American eavesdroppers into believing their navy was still in the North Pacific near Japan itself.

Nevertheless, the U.S. still had a chance to connect dots on December 6, the day before the attack was launched. At noon on that day, the army intercepted and translated a message sent from Tokyo to Ambassador Nomura instructing him to receive an impending 14 part message that was to be considered a counterproposal to American negotiations, and he was instructed to deliver the message to Secretary of State Hull at 1:00 p.m. EST on December 7. As the codebreakers were intercepting that message, President Roosevelt was sending his own communication to Emperor Hirohito, which was delivered on the afternoon of December 6. Part of it read, "I am certain that it will be clear to Your Majesty, as it is to me, that in seeking these great objectives both Japan and the United States should agree to eliminate any form of military threat."

Almost simultaneously, as Roosevelt was sending that personal plea to the emperor, the Navy station on Bainbridge Island intercepted and began transmitting the first 13 parts of the message Tokyo was sending its ambassador in Washington. The message thus reached American officials in Washington around 3:00 p.m., and the Navy's cryptologists began translating it.

Bainbridge Island intercepted the very last part of the message around midnight PST and sent it to Washington, where Army cryptologists decoded it and began sharing the communication. The message was not a formal declaration of war, but it made clear that negotiations were finished, and as a result warnings were sent out to American bases to have their guard up overseas. Unfortunately, Admiral Harold Stark, Chief of Naval Operations, believed that previous warnings had been sufficient for Pearl Harbor to be at a proper alert level, so he didn't bother waking up Admiral Husband Kimmel in Hawaii given that it was the dead of night. Meanwhile, early in the morning of December 7, Army Chief of Staff General George Marshall ordered the dispatch of a potential warning of war: "Japanese are presenting at one p.m. Eastern Standard Time today what amounts to an ultimatum also they are under orders to destroy their code machine immediately Stop Just what significance the hour set may have we do not know but be on alert accordingly Stop." However, Marshall would be out on his Sunday routine and was unavailable for contact until noon, and the Army was suffering technical problems that prevented his warning from reaching Hawaii.

Those who had decoded and seen the Japanese communications would not be surprised when they heard about an attack on December 7, 1941. They would, however, be astonished when they heard where that attack took place. By 9:30 a.m. on Sunday, December 7, 1941, Pearl Harbor was ablaze after it had been smashed by aircraft launched by the carriers of the Japanese navy. Eight battleships had been sunk or badly damaged, 350 aircraft had been knocked out, and over 2,000 Americans were dead. Indelible images of the USS *Arizona* exploding and the USS *Oklahoma* capsizing and floating upside down have been ingrained in the American conscience ever since. In less than an hour and a half, the Japanese had almost wiped out America's entire naval presence in the Pacific.

Incredibly, about a half hour after the attack on Pearl Harbor finished, the Japanese ambassador asked for an appointment to see Secretary of State Hull, and the appointment was scheduled for 1:45 p.m. EST. The Japanese representatives arrived at his office at 2:05 p.m., about 90 minutes after the attack on Pearl Harbor ended, and he delivered the 14 point message to Secretary of State Hull. Although the Japanese ambassador had truly been left in the dark, Secretary Hull was apoplectic upon receiving the message. At that instant he refused to believe that the Japanese ambassador was unaware of what had just happened and proceeded to completely dress him down. Hull reportedly told him, "I must say that in all my conversations with you during the last nine months I have never uttered one word of untruth. This is borne out absolutely by the record. In all my 50 years of public service I have never seen a document that was more crowded with infamous falsehoods and distortions - infamous falsehoods and distortions on a scale so huge that I never imagined until today that any Government on this planet was capable of uttering them."

Secretary Hull

Hours after the attack on Pearl Harbor, the Japanese invaded the Philippines, where American military leaders had anticipated a surprise attack before Pearl Harbor and were almost certain an attack was coming after Pearl Harbor. Even still, the Japanese quickly overran the Philippines. On receiving news of the successful attack at Pearl Harbor, Emperor Hirohito was said to have been "in a splendid mood."

Roosevelt addressed Congress and the nation the following day, giving a stirring speech seeking a declaration of war against Japan. The beginning lines of the speech are instantly familiar, with Roosevelt forever marking Pearl Harbor in the national conscience as "a date which will live in infamy." Congress voted overwhelmingly in support of an immediate declaration of war: 82-0 in the Senate and 388-1 in the House. Churchill had said that Britain would declare war "within the hour" if Japan attacked America. There was no way that the British were going to forget the support they had already received from Roosevelt. Britain was at war with Japan the same day. The other Axis powers quickly followed suit, with Germany and Italy declaring war on America and vice versa by December 11.

The Pacific Theater

Despite fighting in North Africa and the Atlantic, the United States still had the resources and manpower to fight the Japanese in the Pacific. Though the Japanese had crippled the American fleet at Pearl Harbor, its distance from Japan made an invasion of Pearl Harbor impossible, and

Japan had not severely damaged important infrastructure. Thus, the United States was able to quickly rebuild a fleet, still stationed at Pearl Harbor right in the heart of the Pacific. This forward location allowed the United States to immediately push deeply into the Pacific theater.

The war in the Pacific lasted for over three years, and initially, the Japanese forces were extremely successful, conquering Burma, Malaya, Singapore, the Dutch East Indies, Guam, Wake Island and Hong Kong as well as the US held Philippines. Hirohito and the Japanese military leadership were delighted and surprised by the extent of their success. One setback occurred in April when a number of American B-25 bombers launched from the aircraft carrier *Hornet* bombed Tokyo. This stunned the emperor, who had been told that the city was impregnable to US air attacks. Eight American servicemen were captured and sentenced to death by a military tribunal, in defiance of international law covering the treatment of prisoners of war. For unknown reasons, Hirohito intervened and commuted the sentences of five to imprisonment, which was brutal enough that one of them died in captivity. The other three were executed.

In June 1942, Japan suffered its first major military setback when it lost four aircraft carriers, one heavy cruiser, and thousands of sailors and airmen at a battle near Midway Island in the South Pacific. These were catastrophic losses for the Japanese navy, which could ill afford to lose vital aircraft carriers. Details of the scale of the defeat at Midway were kept secret even from the Japanese army, and Hirohito's only response was to hope that the navy would continue to be "bold and aggressive" in its actions despite the defeat.

In August 1942, American forces mounted an attack on Japanese positions on the islands of Tulagi and Guadalcanal. The campaign, which ran until February 1943, was a bitter and protracted struggle that also happened to be a strange and transitional confrontation quite unlike any other in the long Pacific War. In conjunction with the American victory at the Battle of Midway, Guadalcanal represented the crucial moment when the balance of power in the Pacific tipped in favor of the Allies, but the idea that Guadalcanal would be such a significant battle would have come as a surprise to military strategists and planners on both sides.

Nonetheless, by the time the Guadalcanal campaign was underway, it was a confrontation that neither side actively sought, but that both sides came to believe they could not afford to lose. When Allied forces landed on the island, it was an effort to deny the Japanese the use of the island and other nearby islands, but the Japanese defenders fought bitterly in an effort to push them off the island, resulting in a rather unique battle that consisted mostly of a Japanese offensive against Americans that invaded amphibiously and dug in.

While the Americans closed the campaign with a substantial material advantage, the American garrison on Guadalcanal was initially undermanned and terribly undersupplied. Guadalcanal was a stunning blow to the Japanese, who had believed that the United Sates would not be capable of mounting such effective offensive operations until 1943 at the earliest. Hirohito responded by insisting that large numbers of troops and aircraft be moved to the islands to resist the Americans.

Eventually, nearly 100,000 soldiers fought on the island, and the ferocity with which the Japanese fought was a fitting prelude to campaigns like Iwo Jima and Okinawa. The campaign would include six separate naval battles, three large-scale land clashes, and almost daily skirmishing and shelling. Not surprisingly, the campaign exacted a heavy toll, with more than 60 ships sunk, more than 1200 aircraft destroyed, and more than 38,000 dead. While the Japanese and Americans engaged at sea and in the skies, of the 36,000 Japanese defenders on the ground, over 30,000 of them would be dead by the end of the Guadalcanal campaign, while the Americans lost about 7,000 killed.

By the end of the fighting, the Guadalcanal Campaign had unquestionably become a turning point in the Pacific War, representing both the last gasp of the Japanese offensive and the first stirrings of the American onslaught. In the wake of the Japanese defeat, Major General Kiyotake Kawaguchi asserted, "Guadalcanal is no longer merely a name of an island in Japanese military history. It is the name of the graveyard of the Japanese army."

Guadalcanal had been conceived as merely the first and smallest phase of a campaign to capture Japan's southwestern Pacific headquarters in Rabaul, but as the campaign metastasized into an essential win-at-all-costs conflict, concerns over the prize of Rabaul gradually withered away. In the end, the Americans elected to bypass Rabaul. Effectively cut off from contact with the rest of the Japanese war effort, frequently bombarded, alone and impotent, Rabaul was never actually invaded. Instead, the Americans turned their attentions to the north and west, to the Philippines, the Central Pacific, and beyond. Having reached the practical outer limits of their Asian-Pacific empire, and having gambled away so much at Midway and Guadalcanal, the Japanese hunkered down behind an extensive defense perimeter, awaiting the inevitable American advance. Conversely, the Americans, having finally succeeded in mobilizing their massive population and industrial economy on behalf of the war effort, began to overwhelm their Japanese opponents with men and materiel.

By late 1943, the American advance continued across a wide expanse of the Pacific, and it was clear that Hirohito was losing patience with the Japanese military. In an angry exchange, he complained to General Hajime Sugiyama, "Isn't there someplace where we can strike the United States? When and where on earth are you ever going to put up a good fight?"

The string of Japanese military defeats continued throughout 1944. When in June 1944 an American invasion force was spotted heading for the strategically important island of Saipan in the Marianas, the Japanese High Command supported by the emperor created a huge force of warships and aircraft carriers to oppose it. The outcome was one of the most decisive battles of the Pacific Theater and one of Japan's most grievous defeats. Japan lost three aircraft carriers and almost 400 of their dwindling supply of combat aircraft, while the Americans suffered virtually no damage. By mid-July, Saipan had fallen and an American air base was quickly built, from which B-29 bombers could reach the Japanese home islands.

Hirohito's response to the fall of Saipan was similar to his response to other military setbacks: he told the Japanese High Command to produce a plan for a counterattack to recapture the island. This ignored the fact that the Japanese military was no longer strong enough to mount successful large-scale attacks on American forces. The losses in particular of trained pilots and aircraft seriously weakened the effectiveness of Japanese forces. Hirohito's anger and frustration seemed to be rooted in a failure (or refusal) to accept the realities of Japan's increasingly weak military position. Prince Takamatsu, Hirohito's brother, noted in his diary, "The emperor doesn't realize the gravity of the situation; he cleaves rigidly to bureaucratic hierarchy and is liable to dismiss anyone who steps beyond his jurisdiction."

Hirohito seemed to continue to believe that the war could still be won well after most of his military leaders had recognized that defeat was inevitable. Japan's allies in Europe, Italy and Germany, were also in trouble by 1943. The Nazis had been pushed out of Africa, the Red Army was rolling west after bitterly holding on at places like Stalingrad and Leningrad, and Italy had capitulated in late 1943 after the Allied invasion of Sicily. In June 1944, the amphibious landing at Normandy meant that Germany was facing war on three separate fronts across Europe.

When Admiral Chester Nimitz was directed to capture an island in the Bonin group, Iwo Jima stood out for its importance in making progress against the mainland, with three airfields that would allow American air forces to attack the Japanese mainland. But the Japanese were also fully aware of how important Iwo Jima was, and they fought desperately in bunkers and tunnels that required the Americans to carefully clear them out gradually.

The Battle of Iwo Jima, codenamed "Operation Detachment," is more of a misnomer than anything. It was fought as part of a large American invasion directed by steps toward the Japanese mainland, and it was more like a siege that lasted 36 days from February-March 1945, with nonstop fighting every minute. In fact, the iconic flag-raising photo was taken just four days into the battle, and as that picture suggests, the battle was not a pristine tactical event but an unceasing horror with no haven for protection. As veteran and author James F. Christ put it in the foreword of his exhaustive study of the action, the battle was "carnage…that is what Iwo was…the Gettysburg of the Pacific." Iwo Jima defined the classical amphibious assault of the World War II era, as much as the Normandy invasion did, but it came later in the war. In Europe, the Battle of the Bulge had already been won, and German forces would surrender in early May. However, the Japanese Empire was still at a considerable level of strength and state of resolve, and the American offensive, grinding from island to island with naval unit to naval unit and air to air, was met with maniacal resistance by the Japanese. Less than 5% of the Japanese soldiers on Iwo Jima were taken alive, and American casualties were estimated at 26,000, with 6,800 killed or captured.

Near the end of 1944, as Allied forces were pushing across the Pacific and edging ever closer to Japan, plans were drawn up to invade the Ryuku islands, the most prominent of them being Okinawa. Military planners anticipated that an amphibious campaign would last a week, but instead of facing 60,000 Japanese defenders as estimated, there were closer to 120,000 on the island at the beginning of the campaign in April 1945. The Battle of Okinawa was the largest amphibious operation in the Pacific theater, and it would last nearly 3 months and wind up being the fiercest in the Pacific theater during the war, with nearly 60,000 American casualties and over 100,000 Japanese soldiers killed. In addition, the battle resulted in an estimated 40,000-150,000 Japanese civilian casualties.

Okinawa witnessed every conceivable horror of war both on land and at sea. American ground forces on Okinawa had to deal with bad weather (including a typhoon), anti-tank moats, barbed wire, mines, caves, underground tunnel networks, and fanatical Japanese soldiers who were willing to use human shields while fighting to the death. Allied naval forces supporting the amphibious invasion had to contend with Japan's notorious kamikazes, suicide pilots who terrorized sailors as they frantically tried to shoot down the Japanese planes before they could hit Allied ships. As one sailor aboard the USS *Miami* recalled, "They came in swarms from all directions. The barrels of our ship's guns got so hot we had to use firehoses to cool them down." As *The Marine Corps Gazette* noted, "More mental health issues arose from the Battle of Okinawa than any other battle in the Pacific during World War II. The constant bombardment from artillery and mortars coupled with the high casualty rates led to a great deal of men coming down with combat fatigue. Additionally the rains caused mud that prevented tanks from moving and tracks from pulling out the dead, forcing Marines (who pride themselves on burying their dead in a proper and honorable manner) to leave their comrades where they lay. This, coupled with thousands of bodies both friend and foe littering the entire island, created a scent you could nearly taste. Morale was dangerously low by the month of May and the state of discipline on a moral basis had a new low barometer for acceptable behavior. The ruthless atrocities by the Japanese throughout the war had already brought on an altered behavior (deemed so by traditional standards) by many Americans resulting in the desecration of Japanese remains, but the Japanese tactic of using the Okinawan people as human shields brought about a new aspect of terror and torment to the psychological capacity of the Americans."

Given the horrific nature of the combat, and the fact that it was incessant for several weeks, it's no surprise that Okinawa had a profound psychological effect on the men who fought, but it also greatly influenced the thinking of military leaders who were planning subsequent campaigns, including a potential invasion of the Japanese mainland. The casualty tolls at Okinawa ultimately helped compel President Truman to use the atomic bombs on Hiroshima and Nagasaki in an effort to end the war before having to attempt such an invasion.

As these efforts were going on, the emperor once again illustrated his disconnection with military realities by angrily demanding, "Why doesn't the field army go on the offensive?" The answer was simple: the field army no longer had the resources or troops to mount an effective counterattack anywhere. Japanese troops, often short of food and ammunition, defended every position fanatically, but they could not stop the inexorable American advance.

Most members of the Japanese leadership recognized that the war could no longer be won, but the majority were in favor of continuing to fight in hopes that Japan could attain a level of military strength that would allow advantageous peace negotiations. The emperor certainly seemed to believe that it was still possible for Japanese forces to win significant victories, telling an imperial conference in February 1945 that "if we hold out long enough in this war, we may be able to win."

In March 1945, several hundred American bombers took part in the first incendiary bombing attack on Tokyo, which left large sections of the city devastated. After the Nazis surrendered, it left Japan alone to face American and British forces, which were beginning to be transferred from Europe. By the end of June, even the emperor seemed to accept that defeat was inevitable, and he agreed to the beginning of diplomatic moves to negotiate, though there was no consideration of surrender.

On June 22, the Battle of Okinawa officially concluded as American troops finally controlled the entire island, but Okinawa has remained an endless source of both fascination and controversy. One of the most notable aspects of the battle was the Japanese's determination to fight to the death, but they also forced civilians into fighting and even forced civilians to commit mass suicide when the end was near. A recent documentary has asserted "there were two types of orders for 'honorable deaths' - one for residents to kill each other and the other for the military to kill all residents." As a result, it's believed that over 100,000 civilians may have been killed, a number made all the more difficult to estimate due to the fact that an untold number evacuated into caves and were entombed in them when American soldiers sealed them as they advanced in order to protect themselves. American troops also used flamethrowers to smoke the Japanese out of caves, and in the process, it was impossible to distinguish civilians from soldiers.

Most importantly, the Battle of Okinawa was so ruthless that it convinced Allied leaders that the invasion of Japan would be an absolute bloodbath for all sides. American military officials estimated that there would be upwards of a million Allied casualties if they had to invade the Japanese mainland, and if they were successful, Japan would suffer tens of millions of casualties in the process. As the Battle of Okinawa was about to finish, America's secret Manhattan Project was on the brink of its final goal: a successful detonation of a nuclear device. On July 16, 1945, the first detonation of a nuclear device took place in Alamogordo, New Mexico.

Before making his decision to use the bomb, President Harry Truman considered some of the ethical advice submitted by American physicists, particularly the idea of warning the Japanese to surrender before using a nuclear weapon. At the Potsdam Conference on July 26th, the U.S., the United Kingdom and China issued the Potsdam Declaration, giving the Japanese an ultimatum to surrender or suffer "prompt and utter destruction."

Japan chose to ignore the ultimatum, and ultimately Truman chose to use the bombs. Truman took ethical concerns into account, but the deadly experience of Okinawa made clear that hundreds of thousands of Americans would be casualties in a conventional invasion of the mainland of Japan. Moreover, the fanatical manner in which Japanese soldiers and civilians held out on Okinawa indicated that the Japanese would suffer more casualties during an invasion than they would if the bombs were used. Thus, pursuant to the Quebec Agreement, Canada and Great Britain consented to the use of the bomb, and as a result, Truman authorized its use on two sites in Japan.

On August 6, 1945, an American B-29 bomber dropped a nuclear weapon on the city of Hiroshima. The city was virtually destroyed, around 150,000 people were killed immediately, and up to 100,000 more died from the effects of radiation. Three days later, another nuclear weapon was dropped on the city of Nagasaki.

The atomic bombings of Hiroshima and Nagasaki in August 1945 also remain controversial, but one of the most telling facts about the events that ended the war in the Pacific is that more Japanese died at Okinawa than in both atomic bombings combined.

The day after the attack on Nagasaki, at the insistence of the emperor and against the wishes of most military leaders, Japanese High Command issued a communiqué which noted that Japan was ready to consider surrender, with one significant proviso: it rejected "any demand which prejudices the prerogatives of His Majesty as a Sovereign Ruler." Hirohito was willing to consider surrender, but only if his own position and authority were maintained.

On August 15, 1945 the Japanese people heard their emperor give a radio broadcast in which he told them that Japanese forces would cease fighting. However, even this was couched in terms which suggested anything but a complete surrender in the face of overwhelming military setbacks. Hirohito told his listeners that the war against America had been one of self-defense, and that in ordering Japanese forces to cease fighting, he was acting to save human civilization from extinction and ensure peace for generations to come. This self-serving speech carefully avoided using the words "defeat" or "surrender" and it noted only that the emperor had decided to "effect a settlement of the present situation." Overall, this sounded more like a gracious victory announcement than an admission that Japan had been forced to surrender.

Hirohito and Japan After the War

The very day that Emperor Hirohito announced Japan's surrender, General Douglas MacArthur was appointed as Supreme Commander Allied Powers for Japan. Two weeks later, on August 30, 1945, he flew in to Atsugi air base in what British Prime Minister Winston Churchill described as one of the bravest acts of World War II. Despite the emperor's announcement, Japan was heavily militarized, with no certainty at all that the army would comply with his wishes. The airbase outside Tokyo was held by a skeleton and jumpy force of American Marines, with hundreds of thousands of armed and resentful Japanese troops in the vicinity. The country was a potential powder keg waiting to go off.

MacArthur's handling of this situation over the next few weeks, part and parcel of his compassion and his understanding of Asiatic cultures, ranks as one of his finest achievements. He refused to signal or imply any notion of humiliation with respect to the Japanese people. The famous surrender ceremony on board the *Missouri* was to set the tone for his administration of Japan. Japan had surrendered unconditionally, and the hundreds of Allied aircraft which swept across the skies above the battleship that morning underlined the point, but this was to be a reconciliation and a partnership as well. In the radio broadcast after the surrender ceremony, MacArthur made that much clear, saying, "We stand in Tokyo today reminiscent of our countryman, Commodore Perry, ninety-two years ago. His purpose was to bring to Japan an era of enlightenment and progress, by lifting the veil of isolation to the friendship, trade, and commerce of the world. But alas the knowledge thereby gained of western science was forged into an instrument of oppression and human enslavement. Freedom of expression, freedom of action, even freedom of thought were denied through appeal to superstition, and through the application of force. We are committed by the Potsdam Declaration of principles to see that the Japanese people are liberated from this condition of slavery. ... To the Pacific basin has come the vista of a new emancipated world. Today, freedom is on the offensive, democracy is on the march. Today, in Asia as well as in Europe, unshackled peoples are tasting the full sweetness of liberty, the relief from fear."

MacArthur signing the surrender document on the USS *Missouri*

A similar and skilled message was transmitted by the well-known photograph circulated after his first meeting with the Emperor later that month. A casually dressed and stern-looking MacArthur towers above Hirohito, and the Japanese wanted the picture suppressed, but MacArthur knew what he was doing.

MacArthur and Hirohito

During this time, MacArthur lived at the U.S. embassy and was driven in an unprotected car the five minutes to the Dai Ichi Life Insurance building in the center of Tokyo each day, seven days a week. From there he built a large bureaucracy designed to mirror and direct the existing government departments. Unlike their stance in post-war Germany, the Americans applied a light touch and gradualist approach to those who might be tainted by the recent regime. At the same time, this was not true in the broader areas of public policy, where Japan was to be redesigned from top to bottom.

Most of the important aspects of this strategy were determined by the Truman administration in Washington, with MacArthur as their agent, but he nonetheless proved supremely skillful and in several vital areas he acted independently, sometimes in contradiction of orders.[16] The most obvious example was that of food distribution. U.S. Army supplies were not to be distributed to the Japanese, but as the man on the ground, MacArthur appreciated the immediate threat of

---

[16] Frank describes his role as that of a conductor interpreting a brilliant but incomplete musical score (e book location 2904).

serious famine. His swift decision to distribute food and to insist on massive resupplies from back home is now believed to have saved literally millions of lives. It is a major reason why, to this day, many in Japan refer fondly to MacArthur as *Gaijin Shogun* ("Foreign General").

The Americans reconstructed Japan with far more than food. American medical services preempted a 1946 cholera epidemic and introduced basic hygiene and medical standards across the country, potentially saving millions. In October, a Bill of Rights was imposed, triggering the resignation of the government. MacArthur did not care - Shidehara was installed to replace Prime Minister Higashikuni and the redesign of the country continued. In December, Shinto was disestablished as a state religion. At a stroke, Emperor Hirohito lost his status as a divine figure.

There was to be a new constitution as well. Though mostly dictated by Washington, it was MacArthur who personally drafted the famous Article IX, precluding Japanese re-armament. A Westminster model was introduced with the emperor serving as notional head of state. Throughout World War II, public opinion in America seems to have been predicated on the notion that victory would see the removal of the Japanese emperor. After all, he had seemed to enthusiastically support the war, and as people became more aware of the long-term, systematic brutality the Japanese inflicted on prisoners of war and civilians in conquered areas, it seemed logical to assume that the emperor would be held responsible to some degree and removed from power. Several allied countries clearly felt the same way, and New Zealand's prime minister publicly stated his belief that the Japanese emperor should be tried as a war criminal.

Indeed, the American stance toward Hirohito represented another of MacArthur's interventions. Although he had been told to prepare a prosecution case against him, MacArthur argued strongly against indicting Hirohito as a war criminal, even if this meant suppressing potential evidence against him: "His indictment will unquestionably cause a tremendous convulsion among the Japanese people, the repercussions of which cannot be overestimated. Destroy him and the nation will disintegrate…It is quite possible that a million (US) troops would be required which would have to be maintained for an indefinite number of years." He was probably right, and throughout his tenure in Japan he displayed an astonishing sense of just how far and how fast change could be pushed through.

Indeed, the constitution imposed by the Americans was completely radical to the Japanese. Women were enfranchised, while child labor and feudalism were abolished. The land reform that followed saw the 10% of farms owned by those working on them rise to 89% within two years. Trade union membership, another one of Washington's ambitions, also soared. In 1951, MacArthur would boast to Congress, "The Japanese people since the war have undergone the greatest reformation recorded in modern history. With a commendable will, eagerness to learn, and marked capacity to understand, they have from the ashes left in war's wake erected in Japan an edifice dedicated to the supremacy of individual liberty and personal dignity, and in the ensuing process there has been created a truly representative government committed to the advance of political morality, freedom of economic enterprise, and social justice."

America's occupation of Japan in the late 1940s was not all benign. The democracy they were hoping to inculcate, supported by the complete overhaul of society, was hardly introduced consensually. The war trials that followed Japan's surrender were also questionable, given the broader policy ambition. "Judges" from the U.S. Army, without any legal background, made life or death rulings. General Yamashita, who had commanded in the Philippines, was held responsible for the Manila massacre despite the fact that Iwabuchi had ordered it and Yamashita, in another sector, had probably not even known about it.[17] MacArthur nevertheless refused to offer him clemency.

Despite Japan's much vaunted post-war economic rise, it was in this area that the American administration was perhaps least effective. Attempts to reform the powerful Zaibatsu, a group of clannish and incredibly powerful organizations that dominated the economy, were largely circumvented. More importantly, in 1949 banker Joseph Dodge was appointed by Truman to shrink Japan's debt and America's commitment. His radical deflation crippled the economy. MacArthur was completely opposed to this strategy, but by this time his influence was waning.

What saved Japan's economy and propelled MacArthur towards an entirely different challenge occurred 800 miles away. On June 25, 1950, North Korean tanks surged across the 38th parallel, starting the Korean War. As that indicated, the Cold War threatened to turn hot as communists looked to overrun countries across the world, and the Truman administration believed the West would need a strong Japan as a bulwark against further Russian expansion.

With the emperor at the heart of Japanese society, it became clear that it might be better for America to nominally keep Hirohito in power, and to justify that, it was necessary for the Americans to create a new account of the emperor's role in World War II. For their part, this was something that Hirohito and a large section of the Japanese leadership seemed very happy to accept. In the period between the surrender and the arrival of American forces to establish the administration of occupation in Japan, there was a concerted effort to destroy documents related to the emperor's knowledge of the use of poison gas, the execution of prisoners of war, the forced sexual slavery of large numbers of women from conquered territories, and the deaths of somewhere between 10-20 million people in China as a direct result of Japanese military actions. There were also efforts to destroy documents demonstrating the emperor's direct control over the military.

From the day of surrender onwards, Hirohito did not appear in public in any military uniform, something he had done virtually all the time since he had become emperor. On January 1, 1946, the emperor issued a New Year rescript in which he seemed to suggest that the war was the fault

---

[17] Iwabuchi had committed suicide as the city fell.

of a small, aggressive faction within the Japanese High Command. The statement was clearly an attempt to create a new version of Hirohito's leadership during World War II. General MacArthur noted that "the emperor's New Year's statement pleases me very much. By it he undertakes a leading part in democratization of his people. He squarely takes his stand for the future along liberal lines."

Reading the actual text of the rescript does not show any of these things, but MacArthur was making it clear that Emperor Hirohito would not be regarded as a war criminal. Several hundred low-level Japanese were executed for war crimes in the period immediately following the end of the war, and a trial of more senior leaders dragged on until late 1948. In that time, Tojo Hideki, the former Minister of War, and six other defendants were sentenced to death and executed for war crimes including the violation of international law and ordering the inhumane treatment of prisoners of war and others. MacArthur ensured that there was no mention of the emperor during the trial and no suggestion that he too could have been prosecuted for the same offenses.

Thus, an expedient myth was created that portrayed Emperor Hirohito as a helpless pawn who was controlled by a ruthless and determined faction within the Japanese military. This suited the Americans, who were keen to see Japan rebuilt under democratic principles as quickly as possible. Hirohito went along with this, issuing a statement in March 1946 about his role during the war. It claimed, among other things, that he had been "a virtual prisoner and was powerless." This was patently untrue, but it was better to make believe. According to American historian John W. Dower, "This successful campaign to absolve the emperor of war responsibility knew no bounds. Hirohito was not merely presented as being innocent of any formal acts that might make him culpable to indictment as a war criminal, he was turned into an almost saintly figure who did not even bear moral responsibility for the war."[18]

Although the emperor remained very important in post-war Japan, his direct role in government was reduced almost to nothing. Like many other constitutional monarchs, Hirohito became largely a ceremonial figurehead, a focus for a new national identity rather than someone directly involved in running the country. This was formalized in 1947 by the new constitution, which removed virtually all the emperor's influence in politics and the military and made the elected government the heart of power.

When America became involved in the Korean War in 1950, Japan was important as a supply base for American forces. By the time that war ended in 1953, the priority for America had become the prevention of the spread of Communism, and the occupation of Japan ended, though the Americans retained several military bases there.

When the occupation ended, many people seemed to expect that Emperor Hirohito would

---

[18] Dower, John W. *Embracing Defeat: Japan in the Aftermath of World War II*, W. W. Norton and Company, 1999, p. 326.

abdicate in favor of his son, Crown Prince Akihito. Despite the attempt to whitewash the emperor's involvement in World War II, there were still many in Japan and elsewhere who felt that he was still too associated with the war to be effective even as a figurehead. Crown Prince Akihito, by contrast, had no involvement with Japanese military leaders during World War II and had received a Western education. However, Hirohito chose to remain as emperor.

Hirohito and Crown Prince Akihito in 1959

After initial instability in the 1950s, in the 1960s Japan entered a period of astonishing economic growth now referred to as its "economic miracle." The population of Japan grew exponentially, and the country's gross domestic product (GDP) grew by an average of close to 10% each year from 1956-1975. Industrialization expanded, and the portion of the Japanese population living in rural areas declined from around 50% to less than 15%.

During this period of growth, Emperor Hirohito maintained a strong public presence in Japan, including undertaking public "walkabouts" during which he met with ordinary people and made appearances at public events and ceremonies. He also became involved in diplomacy (though only as directed by the Japanese Cabinet) and traveled abroad to meet with a number of world leaders, including President Gerald Ford and Queen Elizabeth II.

The emperor was also able to take the time to indulge his personal fascination for marine biology. In 1925, with the assistance of his mentor, Professor Hirotaro Hattori, the emperor had a marine biology laboratory constructed on the grounds of the Akasaka Palace where he could carry out research. This aspect of the emperor's life was not known in Japan until after the war, when it was felt that the image of the emperor as a scientist would help to make a connection with modernity and a new way of life. He continued to take an active role in research until the mid-1980s, and his son, Crown Prince Akihito, shared his father's interest and gained an international reputation as an ichthyologist.

However, World War II and ongoing questions about the emperor's role in the conduct and prosecution of that war continued to dog Hirohito for the rest of his life. While being interviewed by a journalist for a Japanese newspaper in the 1970s, the emperor was asked whether he felt any responsibility for Japan's involvement in the war. He answered evasively, "I can't answer that kind of question because I haven't thoroughly studied the literature in this field, and so don't really appreciate the nuance of your words."[19]

Hirohito continued to avoid making any direct statement about his role in the war for the rest of his life, but there is some evidence that he may have been privately tormented by continuing questions inside and outside Japan. In 2018, a diary said to have been kept by Shinobu Kobayashi, chamberlain to the Royal Household in the 1980s, was released, and it contained a number of quotes which seemed to give a clue to the emperor's state of mind. In one extract, the emperor was quoted as saying, "I have experienced the deaths of my brother and relatives and have been told about my war responsibility." In the most telling extract of all, a quote from April 1987, Hirohito seemed to welcome death as an escape from the burden of guilt: "There is no point in living a longer life by reducing my workload. It would only increase my chances of seeing or hearing things that are agonizing."

On January 7, 1989 Emperor Hirohito died in his sleep at the Royal Palace in Tokyo following an 18-month battle with cancer. He was 87. Following a lavish state funeral, he was buried in the Musashi Imperial Graveyard in the city of Hachiōji on February 24. He was succeeded as emperor by Crown Prince Akihito.

It is inevitable that the reign of Emperor Hirohito will be mainly remembered for unanswered questions about his responsibility for Japan's role in World War II and for the brutal treatment of prisoners of war and civilians by Japanese forces during that conflict. There are two extreme positions that people continue to take. Some consider Hirohito a dictator who closely controlled the armed forces of Japan, while others insist he was a helpless figurehead who was cynically manipulated by those forces.

The truth seems to lie somewhere between these extremes. In the 1930s, there was a faction within the Japanese military and particularly in the Kwantung Army which appeared to be completely out of the control of the Japanese government and intent on conquering as much of

---

[19] Hebert P. Bix, "Showa History, Rising Nationalism, and the Abe Government," *The Asia-Pacific Journal*, Vol. 13, Issue. No. 2, No. 4, December 2015.

Manchuria as possible. The emperor, like most other senior politicians and some military leaders, found out what this army was doing only after the event. In that sense at least, Hirohito was helpless as this army pursued its own course and extreme factions within the army and navy carried out assassinations in order to destabilize the government. However, the emperor made no attempt to speak out about these things, appearing to be concerned only that Japanese military actions were ultimately successful. In the period immediately before and during World War II, there seems no doubt that Hirohito was directly and actively involved in planning at the highest levels. He intervened in strategic and tactical planning decisions, arbitrated in disputes between high-level leaders, and sent his aides to the front to report back to him. In some cases, such as during the American invasion of Saipan, he actively encouraged commanders to keep on fighting long after they had recognized the situation was hopeless.

The attempt after the war to portray Hirohito as a pacifist who was against the war with America does not tally with the known facts. Hirohito did not directly bring about the war, but the few records which survived appear to show that he enthusiastically supported it, at least in its early and successful stages. No one has been able to produce evidence that Hirohito knew about the testing of biological weapons on prisoners of war, but he was certainly aware of policies which led to the execution of prisoners, and it is almost impossible to believe that he was unaware of atrocities committed by the Japanese military in Nanking. There is no evidence that he ever censured the military for such crimes, and despite international pressure, Emperor Hirohito never issued a formal apology for Japan's actions during World War II. Documents discovered in 2019 suggest that, in a speech to mark the end of the American occupation in 1953, Hirohito planned to use the word "remorse" in a speech about his role in the war. However, he was dissuaded from doing so by Prime Minister Shigeru Yoshida, who felt that this might be interpreted as an admission of responsibility.

There is great irony in the fact that the American occupation and the Japanese leadership colluded after the war to portray Emperor Hirohito as nothing more than a puppet buffeted by forces beyond his control. The irony lies in the fact that this was precisely what he became for the last 40 years of his reign, leaving him unable to talk openly about things that apparently troubled him deeply. Moreover, those decisions have made it difficult for modern historians to determine what the emperor's true role was in Japan's aggressive expansion in the 1930s and early 1940s. Most Japanese don't seem to want to discuss the war, Japanese political leaders still strenuously try to avoid mentioning it, and during his life, the emperor carefully avoided answering questions about it. The systematic destruction of documents immediately after the Japanese surrender and the fact that most participants are now dead means that there will probably never be a final answer.

In the end, the current consensus seems to be that the emperor was neither a helpless puppet nor an all-powerful dictator, but something between those two extremes. It does seem that he was privately troubled by feelings of guilt and remorse for the remainder of his life, but he was prevented from publicly expressing these. Thus, even as outsiders continue to view him with a mixture of skepticism and contempt, many Japanese admire Hirohito for providing stability and continuity at the very moments Japan needed such things, regardless of his involvement in some of the country's darkest events.

Online Resources

Other books about Japanese history by Charles River Editors

Other books about Hirohito on Amazon

Bibliography

Behr, Edward (1989). Hirohito: Behind the Myth. New York: Villard. ISBN 9780394580722. A controversial book that posited Hirohito as a more active protagonist of World War II than publicly portrayed; it contributed to the re-appraisal of his role.

Herbert P. Bix (2000). Hirohito And The Making Of Modern Japan. Harper. ISBN 978-0-06-019314-0. Winner of the 2001 Pulitzer Prize for General Non-Fiction and the 2000 National Book Critics Circle Award for Biography.

Dower, John W. Embracing Defeat: Japan in the Aftermath of World War II, W. W. Norton and Company, 1999; awarded Pulitzer Prize and National Book Award.

Drea, Edward J. (1998). "Chasing a Decisive Victory: Emperor Hirohito and Japan's War with the West (1941–1945)". In the Service of the Emperor: Essays on the Imperial Japanese Army. Nebraska: University of Nebraska Press. ISBN 978-0-8032-1708-9. online at Questia

Fujiwara, Akira, Shōwa Tennō no Jū-go Nen Sensō (Shōwa Emperor's Fifteen-year War), Aoki Shoten, 1991. ISBN 4-250-91043-1 (Based on the primary sources)

Hidenari, Terasaki Shōwa tennō dokuhakuroku, Bungei Shūnjusha, 1991

Edwin Palmer Hoyt (1992). Hirohito: The emperor and the Man. Praeger Publishers. ISBN 978-0-275-94069-0.

Toshiaki Kawahara (1990). Hirohito and His Times: A Japanese Perspective. Kodansha America. ISBN 978-0-87011-979-8.

Laquerre, Paul-Yanic Showa: Chronicles of a Fallen God, ISBN 978-1729431597 ASIN: B00H6W4TYI

Mosley, Leonard Hirohito, Emperor of Japan, Prentice-Hall, Englewood Cliffs, 1966. ISBN 1-111-75539-6 ISBN 1-199-99760-9, The first full-length biography, it gives his basic story.

Richard Arthur Brabazon Ponsonby-Fane (1959). The Imperial House of Japan. Ponsonby Memorial Society.

Wetzler, Peter (1998). Hirohito and War: Imperial Tradition and Military Decision Making in Prewar Japan. University of Hawaii Press.

Free Books by Charles River Editors

We have brand new titles available for free most days of the week. To see which of our titles are currently free, click on this link.

Discounted Books by Charles River Editors

We have titles at a discount price of just 99 cents everyday. To see which of our titles are currently 99 cents, click on this link.

Made in the USA
Coppell, TX
21 September 2020